Two
Slapstick Biographies

- ONCE UPON A TIME! *A Story of the Brothers Grimm*
- QUICK, ANNIE, GIVE ME A CATCHY LINE!
  A Story of Samuel F.B. Morse

Written and illustrated by

Robert Quackenbush

ROBERT QUACKENBUSH STUDIOS
P.O. Box 20651, NY, NY 10021-0072

Printed in the United States of America.

10 9 8 7 6 5 4 3 2 1

Original **Library of Congress Catologing in Publication Data**

Quackenbush, Robert M.
  Once Upon a Time!

  Summary: Recounts the lives of two German brothers
who collected folktales such as "Hansel and Gretel"
and "Rumpelstiltskin" in order to preserve them for future generations.
    1. Grimm, Jacob, 1785-1863---Juvenile literature.
  2. Grimm, Wilhelm, 1786-1859---Juvenile literature.
  3. Philologists---Germany---Biography---Juvenile
  literature. [1. Grimm, Jacob, 1785-1863. 2. Grimm,
  Wilhelm, 1786-1859. 3. Philologists] I. Title
  PD63.Q3 1985   398.2'1'0922[B] [920]   85-9410
  ISBN 0-13-634536-0

Quackenbush, Robert M.
  Quick, Annie, give me a catchy line!

  Summary: A brief biography of the inventor of the
world's first practical telegraph system.
    1. Morse, Samuel Finely Breese, 1791-1872---
  Juvenile literature. 2. Inventors---United States---
  Biography---Juvenile literature. [1. Morse, Samuel
  Finley Breese, 1791-1872. 2. Inventors] I. Title.
  TK5243.M7Q33 1983 621.382'092'4[B][92]   82-21462
  ISBN 0-13-749762-8

ISBN for this two-books-in-one special edition:
ISBN 0-9612518-1-6

Contents

Once upon a time (this is a true story), there were two brothers named Jacob and Wilhelm Grimm. Jacob was born on January 4, 1785. Wilhelm was born on February 24, 1786. They were the oldest of six children. Being so close in age—just over one year apart—they were like twins. They did everything together. They got up at the same time in the morning, they ate the same breakfast, they read the same books, and they went to bed at the same time every night. They especially liked taking long walks in the country together to collect things like butterflies and birds' eggs. They would trade some of the things they found for things they liked more—like colored stones from their friends' collections. They were born barterers.

Jacob and Wilhelm lived in a house surrounded by cows, chickens, horses, sheep, and cattle in the German town of Hanau. Hanau was in the Kingdom of Hesse-Cassel, which was one of the many kingdoms that divided Germany two hundred years ago (the largest German kingdom was Prussia). The brothers' father was the town clerk of Hanau. He liked nothing better than to wear a uniform and to have his children respond to him in military fashion. Their mother was kindly and hard-working. She always seemed to be sewing new clothes for the children or knitting sweaters for them. The whole family was very close, affectionate, and loyal. They lived during a time of great changes in Europe. It was a time of strife and revolutions and the Napoleonic Wars. In spite of this, or perhaps because of it, the Grimm family was always very interested in their German heritage.

In 1796, when Jacob was eleven and Wilhelm was ten, their father died. Two years later, the brothers moved to the town of Cassel for further schooling; their childhood days were over. When their studies were completed, they decided to study law. They enrolled at Marburg University where Jacob became friends with one of the young instructors, Freidrich Karl von Savigny. Savigny collected books and manuscripts of medieval literature (from about 700 A.D. to 1500). Jacob was in awe of the collection. He spent a great deal of time at the professor's house studying the ancient material. As a result, Savigny invited Jacob to go with him to Paris for a year to research the history of Roman law in the Middle Ages. Jacob gladly accepted the opportunity. But it was the first time that the brothers had been separated. They missed each other terribly. When they were reunited at last, they both swore they would never part again.

11

On October 14, 1806, Napoleon conquered Prussia and all of Germany fell to the French. Napoleon established new order and new thrones. He appointed his brother Jérôme Bonaparte to be king of the new kingdom of Westphalia, which included parts of the kingdom where the Brothers Grimm lived. The royal headquarters was in Cassel. Two years later, in 1808, Jacob and Wilhelm's mother died. Jacob, now twenty-three years old, became head of the family, a position he held for the rest of his life. By now the brothers had finished school. But they did not choose legal careers. They wanted work that would give them time to research old German literature. Luckily, both of them were hired as librarians for the royal library. Their free hours were spent collecting German folksongs and tales, which would later make them famous. Then, through Jacob's friend Savigny, they met Clemens Brentano and Achim von Arnim who also loved the German past and collected ancient literature. Brentano and Arnim invited the brothers to contribute a few of their folksongs to a book called *Wunderhorn* that Arnim was about to publish. By bartering as they had in childhood, Jacob and Wilhelm traded their songs for stories to add to their collection of old tales.

12

The brothers worked together side by side at the same desk and arranged their books for each other's convenience. They continued to collect old tales from family members and friends. Many of the tales, such as *Snow White, Little Red Riding Hood,* and *Sleeping Beauty*, came from Marie Müller; she was the nanny for the Wild family, who owned the only drugstore in Cassel. Some of Marie's tales were French stories that had changed over the years as they were told in German to each new generation of children. In the version told 200 years earlier in France, Little Red Riding Hood was swallowed by the wolf and that was the end of the story. As told by Marie, Red Riding Hood was saved by a woodsman in a happy ending. Marie kept the brothers busy writing down her tales. However, gathering other stories was not so easy. One woman had told some stories to the Grimms' friend Brentano, but he had not written them down. When Jacob and Wilhelm went to see her, she would not tell her stories again because she thought people would laugh at her. Even the brothers' eagerness to barter for the tales could not change her mind.

15

The brothers wandered around the countryside searching for more tales. Under Jacob's careful eye, Wilhelm rewrote the tales, often adding new details. In *Sleeping Beauty*, Marie simply said that everyone fell asleep in the castle, "even the flies on the wall." The remark about the flies gave Wilhelm an idea for expanding the tale. He added what was happening elsewhere in the castle at the precise moment everyone fell asleep. He included horses in the stable, dogs in the courtyard, pigeons on the roof, even the cook who was about to cuff the kitchen boy for a misdeed. The brothers constantly sought to improve the tales and were not yet ready to publish them. Then one day Arnim came to read them. He paraded around the room, dropping page after page on the floor while a pet canary perched comfortably on his head. Arnim insisted that the Grimm brothers publish the collection.

17

In December 1812, the year Napoleon's army met with defeat in Russia, the first volume of *Grimms' Fairy Tales* was published. In writing down the stories, Jacob and Wilhelm had hoped to keep the German heritage alive; they wanted to make their work available for scholars to study. They hadn't given much thought to the children who would enjoy the tales, so they were surprised when families eagerly bought their book to read at home. The brothers quickly set to work on a second collection of tales. This book was much easier to do than the first, because stories came to them from all over. The Grimms didn't have to leave the house. People came pounding on their door with stories. Some knew about the brothers' bartering ways and wanted to trade. The boldest was an old soldier who exchanged his stories for the brothers' old trousers.

19

Grimms' Fairy Tales became popular partly because they helped to restore German national pride. But they also matched the mood of the time. In the Romantic period, people believed that creative powers worked best when the imagination was allowed to flow freely. To escape from the problems of the present, artists and writers turned to faraway places, the medieval past, and the folklore and legends of the common people. Such a movement was appropriate for the troubled times of the Brothers Grimm. So their next volume of tales was eagerly awaited. For the new collection Jacob and Wilhelm had a lucky encounter. They met a genuine storyteller, Frau Katharina Dorothea Viehmann. She lived in a village near Cassel and delivered eggs and butter to friends of the Grimms. Happily for the brothers, she was not a difficult barterer. She settled for rolls and coffee in exchange for her stories.

20

Frau Viehmann told the Grimm brothers more than twenty tales. She had an unequaled gift for retaining the stories firmly in her mind, pure and unspoiled. It was fortunate chance that Jacob and Wilhelm saved her treasure trove of stories, for she died in 1815, only a year after the second volume of fairy tales was published. Her most famous story, *Cinderella*, had evolved from a French tale called *The Little Fur Slipper*. Since the French word for fur, "vair," is similar to the French word for glass, which is "verre," the fur slipper became glass in the second volume of *Grimms' Fairy Tales*. Thanks to Frau Viehmann, the glass slipper went on to make fortunes for the manufacturers of glass slipper novelties for the next hundred and fifty years.

23

The success of the fairy tales brought world-wide fame to the Grimm brothers. They had many visitors: professors, scholars, writers, and the merely curious. The visitors all wanted to meet the famous brothers. One day Hans Christian Andersen came to call. Jacob sent him away. He did not know that Hans Christian Andersen was the famous Danish author of many original tales for children, including *Thumbelina* and *The Little Mermaid*. Wilhelm was not home at the time. When he found out, he was horrified that such an important visitor had been turned away. But Jacob had been busy working on a German grammar book that was to establish his reputation as a philologist—a person who studies literature and its relation to human speech. While he was at work on his grammar book, he had left the collecting of fairy tales to Wilhelm. He had gotten out of touch with people involved in the world of make-believe.

25

On May 15, 1825, thirty-nine-year-old Wilhelm married Dorothea Wild, the druggist's daughter. She was seven years younger than Wilhelm and had been his friend for a long time. The marriage did not change things between Jacob and Wilhelm. Jacob continued to live in the same house with Dorothea and Wilhelm and was a loving uncle to their three children. Wilhelm rose first in the morning to read his Greek testament. At mid-morning he joined Dorothea and Jacob for coffee and then the two brothers went to work—side-by-side—the same as ever. In the afternoon they went for walks together. In the evening they would rejoin the family for supper. This close relationship is revealed by their signing many of their books *Brothers Grimm*. Their name has become a symbol of brotherly friendship and creative cooperation.

27

Second in importance to the *Fairy Tales* was the Grimms' publication of *German Folk Tales*. Folk tales differ from fairy tales because their roots are in reality, a specific place or event in history. Fairy tales are timeless and pure fantasy, often taking place in a medieval setting. Grimms' *Folk Tales* include *The Pied Piper of Hamlin*. This tale is believed to be based on an actual event in history—the Children's Crusade of 1212, when armies of children from Germany and France marched to the Holy Land and were never seen again. By publishing these treasures of German heritage, the brothers brought much honor to their country. However, one person did not think so—Prince William II, ruler of Hesse-Cassel. The German royal family had reclaimed the throne of their kingdom just before Napoleon was defeated at Waterloo in 1815. William II refused to give the brothers the higher salary they requested. Insulted, they accepted an offer from Göttingen University in the Kingdom of Hanover. "So the Grimms are leaving," said William II sarcastically. "What a loss! They have never done anything for me."

ALL WE DID WAS TO ASK FOR A RAISE.

YEAH, AND HE RAISED CAIN.

More misfortune fell upon the Grimms after their move. The Duke of Cumberland had become King of Hanover. He was English and was related to Queen Victoria. He wrote a new constitution for the country. The Grimm brothers and five other scholars and teachers swore loyalty to the old constitution, which the new king wanted to replace. So he had them banished from the kingdom. The Grimms went back to Cassel, where they earned no money for two years. However, they set to work on the first complete dictionary of the German language. It was to serve as the model for dictionaries in other languages. To do the work, the brothers had to refer to huge numbers of books which were stacked on tables and against walls in several rooms. Looking things up meant a lot of work! Fortunately, it did not keep the brothers from forging ahead with their challenging project.

The news of the Grimms' new dictionary reached the King of Prussia. He invited the brothers to come and live in Berlin to work on their dictionary with "the use of all aid and support available." The brothers responded, "We strive for nothing but the opportunity to devote our remaining days to the achievement of the work which relates to the language and history of our beloved fatherland." They moved at once to Berlin. Friends and scholars eagerly awaited their arrival. They moved into a house with ten rooms near a school for Wilhelm's three children, Herman, Rudolf, and Auguste. Soon the house became too small for the active children and the parties they held. The family moved again, but were in the new house only a short time, because Wilhelm forgot to pay the rent while away at a conference. Their final move was to a house next to the railroad station. Suddenly, the brothers, who were used to quiet and solitude and walks in the countryside, liked the hustle and bustle of the big city. They looked forward to living there happily ever after.

꧁ **Epilogue** ꧂

When Jacob died on September 20, 1863, he was buried in Berlin next to his brother Wilhelm who had died four years earlier on December 16, 1859. Like the characters in one of their tales, they had become folk heroes. Their complete writings filled sixty-two volumes. In addition they contributed four books to the thirty-two volume German dictionary that was not completed until 1962. Even so, most people think of them as "The Fairytale Brothers." This is because their best-loved work is *Grimms' Fairy Tales*, which has become a household book in many lands and in seventy languages. In Russia alone over 18,000,000 copies have been sold. About the collection, Wilhelm said, "In the fairy tales a world of magic is opened up before us, one which still exists among us in a secret forest, in underground caves, and in the deepest sea, and is still available to children." But without the Brothers Grimm, the "world of magic" that they preserved would have been lost to us forever.

34

Samuel Finley Breese Morse, born in 1791 in Charlestown, Massachusetts, never did what he was expected to do. While his two younger brothers pored over books like their highly educated father and grandfather, young Samuel would be doing something else. Even when he was sent, in his father's footsteps, at age fourteen to attend college at Yale, Morse kept out of the mainstream. While everyone around him was busy with schoolwork, Morse was dreaming that class was over so he could go painting, drawing, and sketching. Science was about the only subject that held his interest.

37

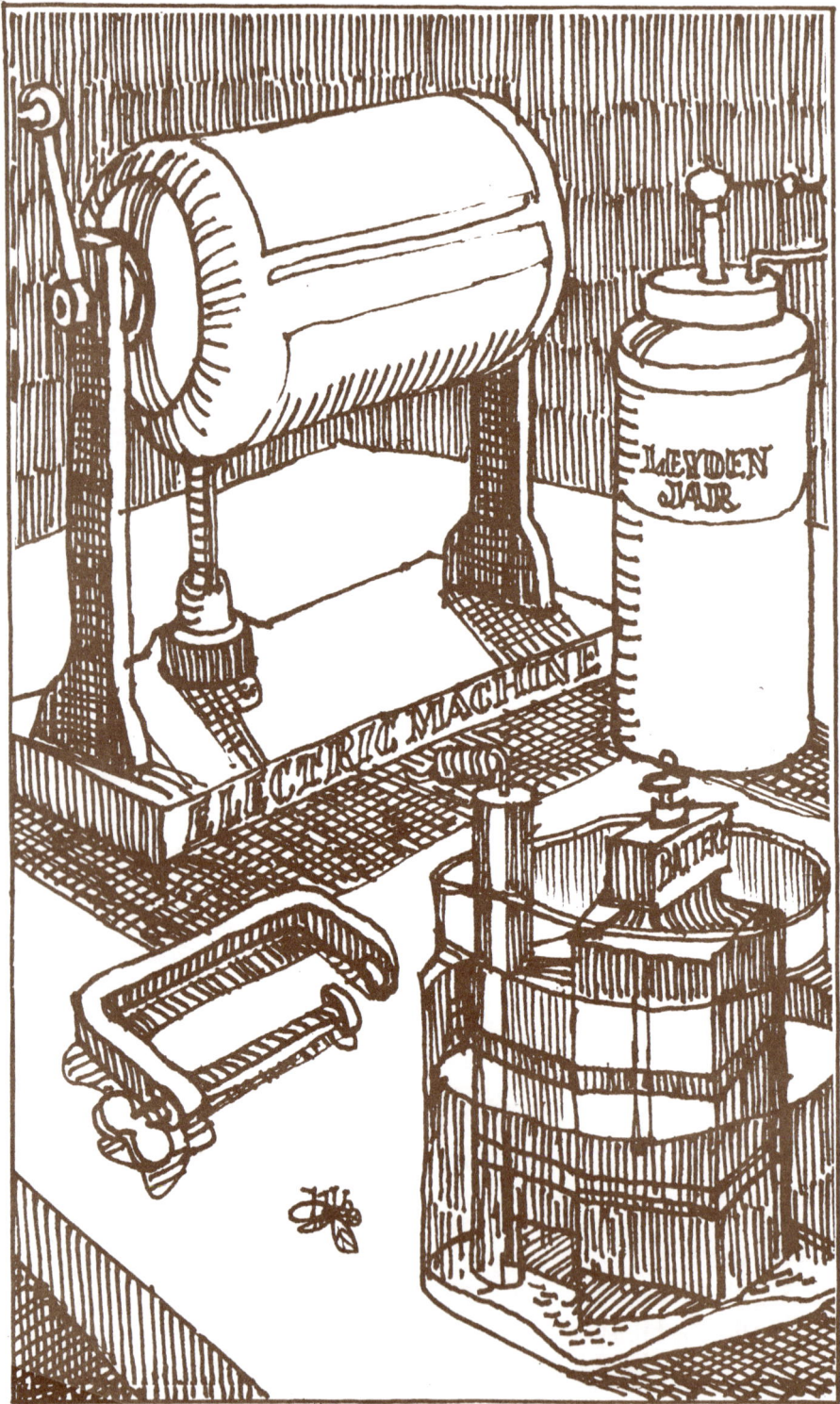

Morse liked science because it was a subject that had just been introduced to American colleges. He was fascinated by some of the classroom experiments. He took apart and reassembled the first kind of battery that had been invented; it contained copper and zinc discs and chemicals that worked together to produce electricity. He also learned about another invention that could store a charge of electricity. It was called a Leyden jar. When the class joined hands in a circle around the jar and the lead man touched the top while the end man touched the side, everyone, simultaneously, received a shock. This proved that electricity flowed in an instantaneous current. But this was about the only "charge" Morse got out of his college days. When he left Yale, at nineteen, he had not prepared himself for a profession.

Morse thought it over and decided he wanted to be an artist. But it was a profession that was almost unheard of in those days. The country was new and most people were poor, so paintings were considered a luxury. Only a few people could earn a living by painting pictures. This did not stop Morse. He went to see two of America's finest painters, Gilbert Stuart and Washington Allston. The two masters thought Morse's work was good; they convinced his parents that he might find a place for himself in the art world. With that, Morse went off with Allston to study in Europe. Four years later, in 1815, he returned to exhibit a group of "history" paintings in Boston. One giant painting, entitled "Dying Hercules," showed the mythical hero lying in agony against a rock. The public would have none of Morse's pictures. Now what was he going to do?

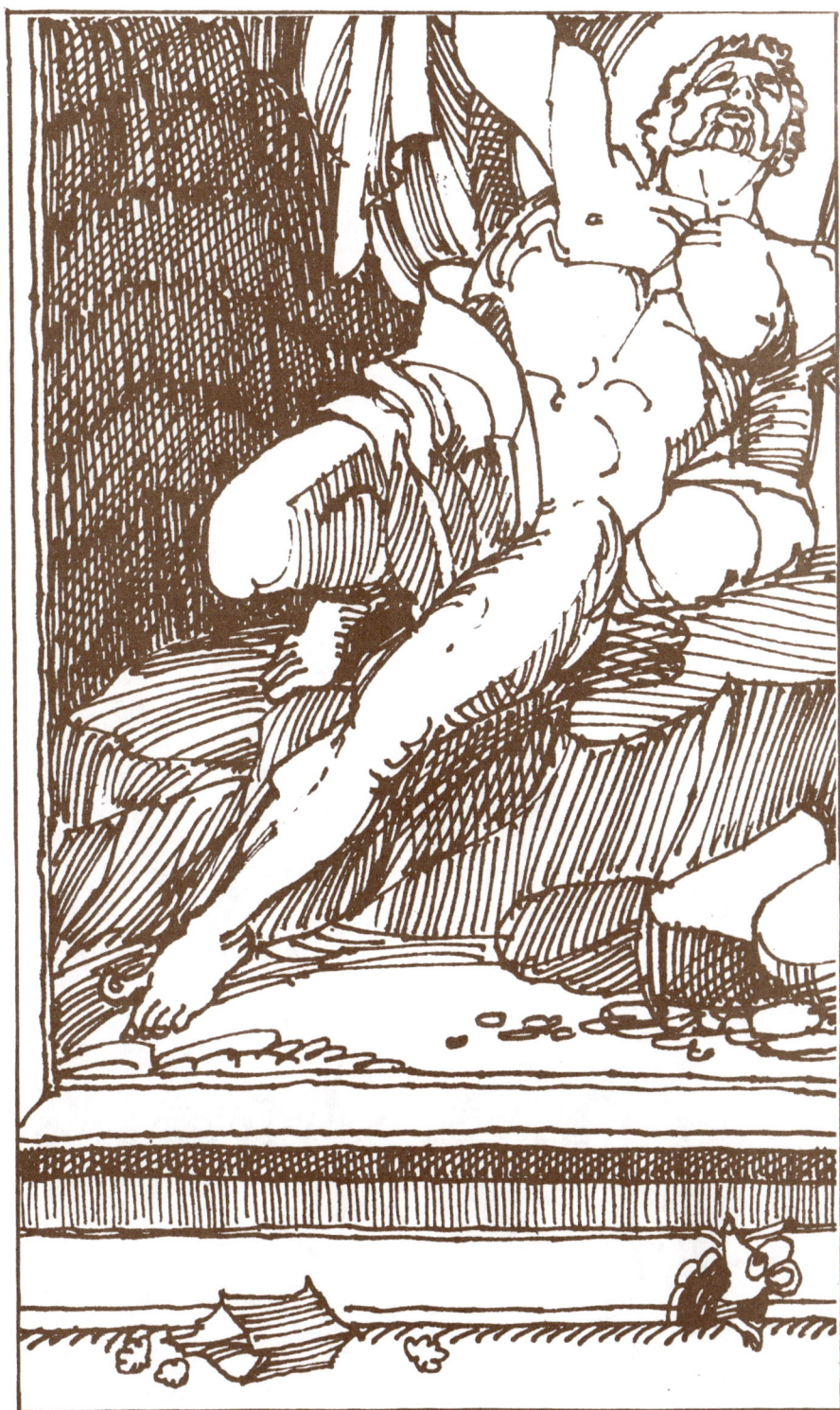

To earn a living, Morse turned to painting portraits. He was not thrilled about doing them, but people seemed to want them. After a few jobs came his way, he settled down and got married. Before long a child was born, and then another. About the time a third child was due, Morse was having trouble finding enough portraits to paint in Boston to support his rapidly growing family. So he sent his wife and children to live with his parents while he took to the road. He went to Albany, New York City, and Charleston, South Carolina, in search of portraits to paint.

43

NOW ON VIEW

HOUSE OF

REPRESEN

PAINTED IN OIL B

SAMUEL F.B. M

By now, twenty years had gone by, and Morse was still struggling to find a rewarding career in art. It was true that he had painted brilliant portraits of Eli Whitney, Daniel Webster, and the Marquis de Lafayette—to name a few. But the portrait commissions didn't come often enough, and when they did they didn't pay enough. And it was also true that he had founded and was head of the National Academy of Design at a time when there were no art galleries, much less art schools, in New York. But this didn't pay, either. He tried all kinds of ways to make money with his art. One time he charged admission for the people of New York to see a giant portrait of Congress he had painted. No one came. In desperation, he decided that a return trip to Europe might change his luck. It didn't. A huge canvas he painted in Paris called "The Gallery of the Louvre," showing dozens of famous paintings mounted on the museum's walls, brought only snubs. Morse headed back home.

45

Returning to the United States in 1832 aboard the packet ship *Sully*, Morse had a conversation in the dining saloon one night that changed his life. A young doctor, Charles T. Jackson, explained how electricity could travel like fluid for miles and miles over a wire. At once Morse was struck with an idea. He could see no reason why a message could not be instantaneously sent over a wire to any distance by electricity. He believed he could invent an instrument to send and receive such messages. He would call it an electric telegraph. For the rest of the voyage he could talk of nothing else. He drove his fellow passengers crazy with his endless talk about an electric telegraph and a code he had devised for it. The code was an alphabet of dots and dashes that could be printed or sounded on a buzzer by opening or closing an electric circuit. But what Morse did not know was that Professor Joseph Henry, a noted physicist, had demonstrated an electric telegraph system in Albany, New York, the year before. In fact, Henry had even published a paper about it.

47

JOSEPH HENRY

BELL

PERMANENT MAGNET

ELECTROMAGNET

WIRE

PIVOT

Joseph Henry had demonstrated his telegraph system by stringing a mile of wire around his classroom. At one end he attached a sending device, or transmitter, hooked up to a battery. At the other end was an iron bar wrapped in wire, called an electromagnet. When the transmitter caused an electric current to go from the battery through the wire to magnetize the bar, the bar caused a permanent magnet to swing on a pivot and ring a small bell. This was the first electromagnetic telegraph. But Henry was more interested in research than in commercial ventures, so he did not bother to have his telegraph patented. This made it possible for Morse to set to work inventing an electromagnetic telegraph of his own. His reason for wanting to invent one was simple. He hoped it would make him rich so he could devote the rest of his life to painting without a worry or care. He did not stop to think that he was going from one impractical profession to another. But that was Morse for you!

49

Morse didn't start working on his telegraph right away. One cause for delay was his decision to run for mayor of New York. He campaigned against almost everything! (Morse's political ideas would seem unacceptable to most people today.) He lost that election and soon ran in another. When he lost the second time, he finally went back to his telegraph and to teaching art at New York University. He built his telegraph out of old canvas stretchers, wooden clock parts, and whatever else he could find around his studio. When it was finished, he energized the system. But it just lay there. Morse poked at this wire and wiggled that one. Still nothing happened. Finally, he begged one of the physicists at the university, Professor Leonard Gale, to take a look at it. Gale was flabbergasted. Morse had wrapped bare uninsulated wire around his magnets. Gale showed him how the magnet and batteries ought to work. He also suggested that Morse study Joseph Henry's published article. Morse needed all the help he could get. So on the spot he took Gale on as a partner.

51

After making the changes Gale suggested and finding out that his telegraph could work, Morse took on a new partner, Alfred Vail. Vail, a former student at the university, agreed to help Morse improve his invention in exchange for one fourth of the profits it would earn. The final result was a machine that was similar to Henry's in principle; however, it could send messages much greater distances. It had what is called a relay. This was an electric battery on the line that would add to the current every time a signal was being sent by a transmitter. This boosted the signal along to a receiver, where it was either transformed to a rat-tat-tat sound or printed on a strip of paper. The message that came out of the receiver, whether it was audible or printed, represented dots and dashes. In turn, these dots and dashes represented letters of the alphabet and became known as the Morse Code.

53

Morse's dedication to the telegraph took more and more time away from his art, until, in 1836, he put down his brushes forever. Two years later, in February 1838, he was invited to give a demonstration of his electric telegraph before the House Committee on Commerce in Washington, D.C. It created a sensation. The committee chairman, Congressman F.O.J. Smith, became Morse's third partner in the telegraph. His task was to launch a bill in Congress that would grant Morse $30,000 to build fifty miles of telegraph. Elated, Morse set sail for Europe to patent his telegraph in as many foreign countries as possible. But he did not have much luck because a telegraph that had been invented by an Englishman, Sir Charles Wheatstone, was already in use in Europe.

55

Morse returned to the United States broke and hungry. He wondered if Congress would *ever* pass his bill. To earn money, he began a new trade he had learned in Europe. He became a teacher of the daguerreotype—one of the earliest forms of photography, made by exposing an image on a plate of chemically treated metal or glass. One of his students was the great Mathew Brady, who years later would become famous for his photographs of the Civil War. But this, too, did not bring in much money, and Morse remained terribly poor. A story is told that when one of his students got behind in his payments, Morse asked when he would be paid. The student answered that he would be paid in one week. Morse replied that he would be dead by then. Quickly, the student rushed Morse out for a meal before it was too late!

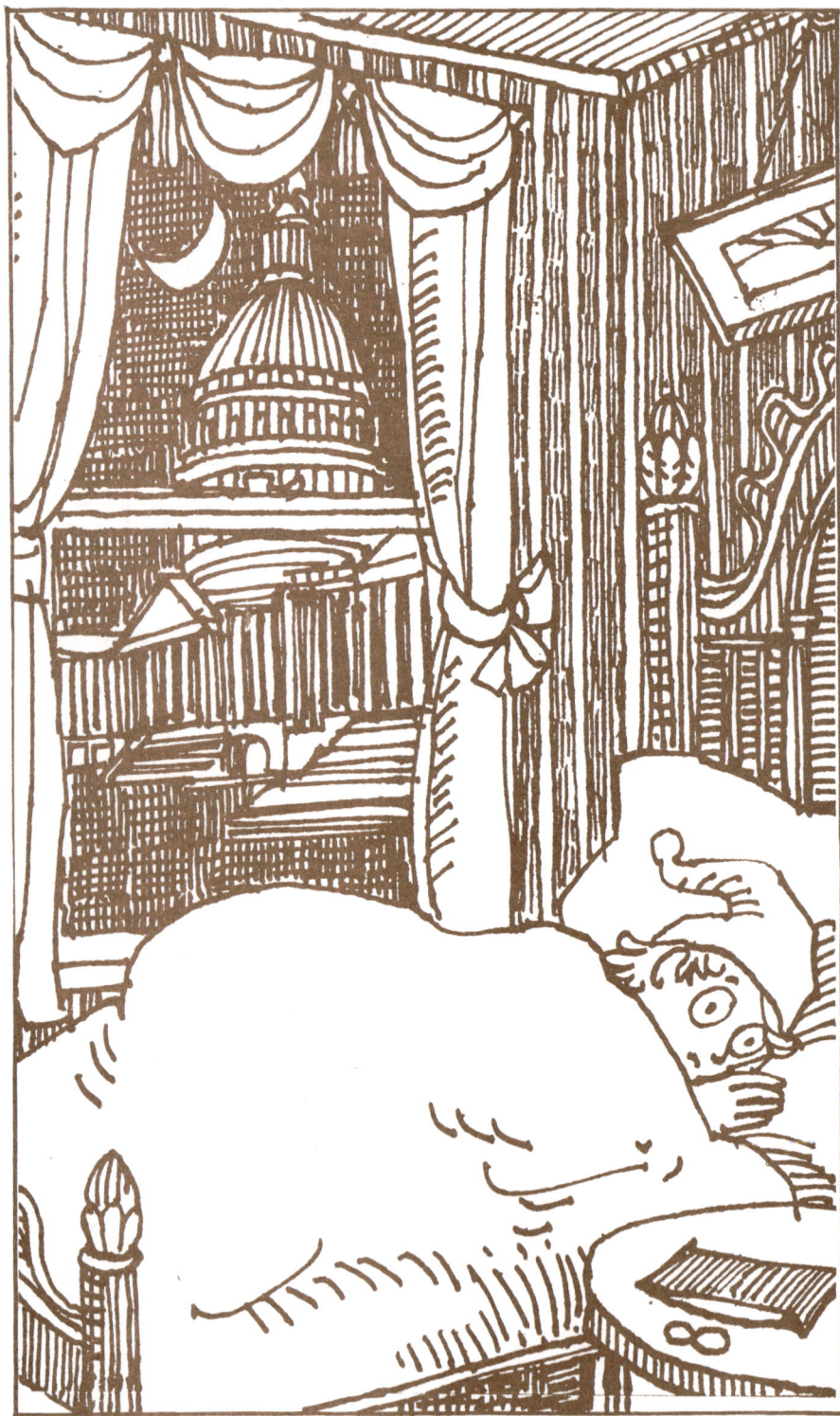

Five more years passed. Morse was still waiting for Congress to pass his bill. If the bill failed, he knew he would be ruined. At last, in February 1843, Congress planned to bring his bill to a vote. Morse checked into a Washington hotel and waited. By the last day of the congressional session, there was still no word. Morse crawled into bed that night knowing that he had just enough money to pay his hotel bill and his train fare back to New York. The next morning there was a knock on his door. Annie Ellsworth, the daughter of a friend, brought Morse tremendous news. Congress had passed his bill 89 to 83, and at midnight President Pierce had signed it! Beside himself with joy, Morse told Annie she could choose the first message that would be sent over his electric telegraph. After some thought, she chose, "What hath God wrought?"

59

The test telegraph line was planned to run right alongside the railroad tracks that stretched forty miles between Washington and Baltimore. The wire was placed in lead pipes and installed underground. But there were problems. It was discovered after nine miles that the electricity would leak from the wire into the ground. The underground operation had to be halted. Morse had spent $23,000 of the money from Congress. There was only $7,000 left. The only thing he could think of was to attach the wire to poles. Twenty-four-foot-tall unbarked chestnut poles were put up every two hundred feet along the tracks. And to save more money, Morse used broken bottle necks at the top of each pole for insulators. On May 24, 1844, the telegraph line was finished, and Annie Ellsworth's message went from Washington to Baltimore. Morse's electromagnetic telegraph was a success!

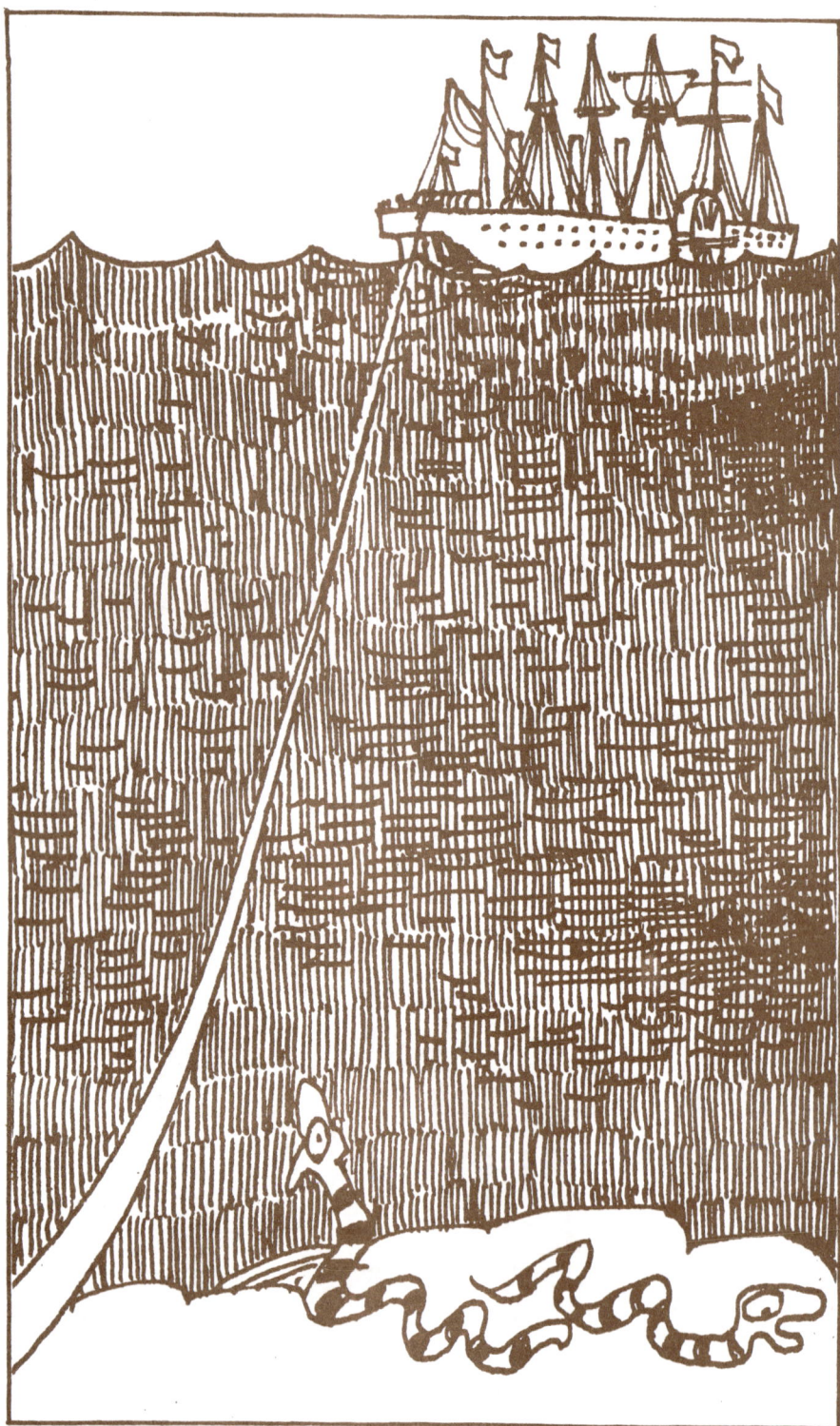

At first, neither Morse nor anyone else knew what to do with the telegraph. But it seemed to take over, in spite of itself. Before long a line was laid across the Atlantic Ocean. Soon a cobweb of Morse's wires covered the world. His telegraph replaced all others—even Wheatstone's, which failed because it made no sound. And so a man who knew hardly anything about electricity and even less about mechanics succeeded in giving the world a practical telegraph system—and got rich at last. After several patent battles over claims by rival inventors, fights with partners, angry quarrels with Professor Henry and with Doctor Jackson, Morse was given full legal credit for inventing the telegraph and was ready to settle down and enjoy his fame and wealth. Ready, that is, but not willing. He could never be like other people, and he drifted back to his absurd politics and other silly pursuits. But that was Morse for you.

🌀🌀 Epilogue 🌀🌀

Many inventors, particularly Joseph Henry, contributed to the invention of the electric telegraph. But it was Morse who had enough determination, interest, and persistence to sell a new device to an indifferent public. For over forty years his telegraph was the world's most important means of long-distance communication. Then came the telephone, the radio, and finally today's satellite TV, which have dimmed the importance of the telegraph. Even so, the name of Samuel F. B. Morse continues to shine for another reason. Today, after nearly one hundred and fifty years, Morse's paintings and portraits are famous, and people across the land flock to see special exhibits of his work at museums and galleries. And the final irony involves "The Gallery of the Louvre," the painting that was ignored by the public in 1832. It was sold by the University of Syracuse in 1982 for the astounding figure of $3,500,000—the highest sum yet paid for an American painter's work.